The BERWICKS COAST

by

Lawson Wood

A Kiss Across the Border.

Stenlake Publishing

1998

FOREWORD

From: Major General Sir John Swinton KCVO OBE JP

Kimmerghame
Duns
Berwickshire
TD11 3LU
Duns (0361) 83277

To the city dweller Berwickshire must seem something of
an anachronism. No zebra has yet to cross our streets, sheep
and cattle easily outnumber our population and our railway
stations disappeared years ago. Only at harvest time does
the roar of combines disturb our peace, though it must
be admitted that the Royal Air Force does its best throughout
the year.

Berwickshire is thrice blessed, with abundant agricultural
land, glorious uplands and a magnificent coastline. It
is on this latter that Lawson Wood has concentrated in
this excellent book.

Already the author of volumes of old picture postcards
on the fishing port of Eyemouth and on the ancient fortified
town of Berwick-upon-Tweed, he has in this volume expanded
his encyclopedic knowledge of the area to include the
whole coastline of Berwickshire from Cockburnspath to
Berwick, and his fascinating postcards are enhanced by
captions containing a wealth of historical information
and local lore.

Whilst the scenes depicted show life as it used to be,
the coast itself has not changed and those who, encouraged
by this book, feel enthused to explore its rugged shore
will not be disappointed.

INTRODUCTION

The Berwickshire coastline stretches from Dunglass Mill at Cockburnspath to Lamberton on the English border. This book follows a route southwards along the 'forgotten coastline', through the picturesque harbour at Cove, past Pease Bay and beyond Fast Castle, made famous by Sir Walter Scott's poem *The Bride of Lammermuir*. The journey continues past Pettico Wick and St Abb's Head to Coldingham Shore, now known as St Abbs, and formerly the site of a cliff-top nunnery. Nearby Coldingham Bay, which witnessed naval action during the last two World Wars, is regarded as one of Europe's finest beaches.

Eyemouth is the largest town on the coast, and much of this book is concerned with her fishing legacy. Burnmouth, to the south, nestles at the base of a steep cliff and is actually made up of four distinct village communities. Lamberton, now on the border, was made famous as the location of the marriage between Princess Margaret Tudor and James IV of Scotland, which united Scotland and England for the first time. The toll house on the border where marriages took place was once more famous than Gretna Green, though sadly none of Lamberton's historic buildings have survived.

Although now part of Northumberland, Berwick-upon-Tweed, which has been claimed by Scotland on many different occasions, is included in the book. The town developed as a seaport for the export of grain, and of course as a result of her fishing industry.

Most of the pictures in this book have been reproduced from postcards, the majority of which were sent between villages only a few miles apart. The distance was often a fraction too far to travel, and in the days of a limited telephone network the postal service was unparalleled.

This book is dedicated to those hardy men and women who carved a living from the land and sea, so many of whom were lost in terrifying circumstances over the years. Where appropriate I have included a few of the old fishermen's songs and prayers. In the words of Peter 'Petie' Hood, a worthy old St Abbs fisherman (as retold to me by my good friend Robbie Nisbet):

If it'll no dae
It'll hae to dae
Whether it'll dae or no.

Lawson Wood, August 1998

© Lawson Wood 1998
First published in the United Kingdom, 1998,
by Stenlake Publishing, Ochiltree Sawmill, The Lade,
Ochiltree, Ayrshire, KA18 2NX
Telephone / Fax: 01290 423114

ISBN 1 84033 046 5

THE PUBLISHERS REGRET THAT THEY CANNOT SUPPLY
COPIES OF ANY PICTURES FEATURED IN THIS BOOK.

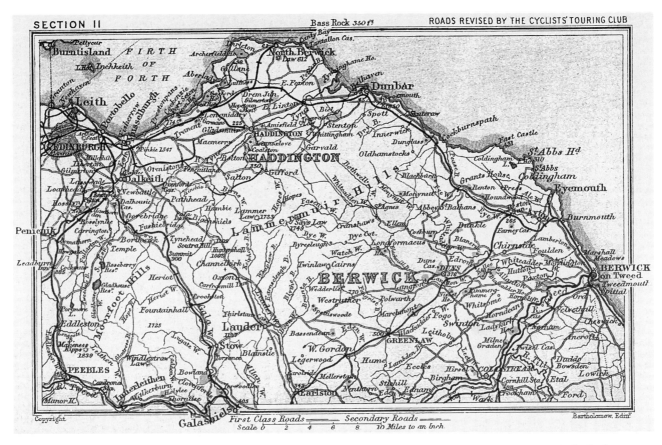

There are many small villages east of the A1 trunk road from Cockburnspath to Berwick-upon-Tweed, all of which are steeped in history, and what better way to illustrate them than through the eyes of the early commercial photographers – the postcard makers. Postcards of maps, such as this one, are quite rare and very collectable.

Dating from 1906, the former Coastguard Station at Cockburnspath is no longer used. The message on this card tells of an itinerant family working with horses and having to stop due to the 'influenza being such a weakening trouble'. The stooks of corn in the foreground would be left in the field to ripen before being fed through the threshing machine.

During both World Wars, Berwickshire's coastal road and rail bridges were guarded to protect them against attack from invaders arriving by sea. Troops also enforced domestic travelling restrictions. These members of the Kings Own Scottish Borderers were seconded to Cockburnspath from the unit's headquarters at the Berwick barracks.

When James IV married Margaret Tudor in 1503, he gave her the lands of Coldbrandspath (Cockburnspath) as part of her dowry. The old mercat cross in the centre of the village, carved with thistles and roses, was put up to commemorate this event. Although James had technically given Cockburnspath to his wife, he subsequently passed it on to William Arnot and his son John Burgess of Edinburgh in lieu of payments for wine!

Carriages used to stop at the Cockburnspath Hotel to change horses before continuing along the Great North Road to Edinburgh or Berwick. A popular stopover, the hotel was quite famous in its heyday. The card showing the horses and carts was posted in 1915. Rather remarkably, the lower picture, dating from *circa* 1900, is postmarked 18 September 1979 and was sent by the US postal service to an address in Maryland with the message 'Congratulations on your 50th'!

COCKBURNSPATH TOWER.

The remains of Cockburnspath Tower, the former home of the Earls of Dunbar and March, lie a little south of Cockburnspath, before Pease Bridge. The tower, which appears as Ravenswood Castle in Sir Walter Scott's *Bride of Lammermuir,* was overrun in 1547 and much of the masonry taken to Eyemouth for the construction of the fort on the headland. Cockburnspath was once a very important castle, and was often visited by royalty and members of the nobility.

Fishermen's Houses, Cove, Cockburnspath.

Cove is a typical 'heugh-heid' (cliff-top) village. Its small community lived principally from the sea, mainly catching crabs and lobsters, although they had allotments for growing vegetables too. The design of the lobster pots, left, remains unchanged today.

Fairbairn & Sons' Store, Cove

Mr Fairbairn and his two sons with produce including rabbits and pheasants. The cart was used to transport lobster pots up and down the brae between the harbour and nearby railway station. The message on this postcard, sent by A. Fairbairn to another member of the family in Dunbar, tells of a forthcoming bazaar. A century ago, haddock, whiting, cod, skate, halibut and herring would have been sold by the Fairbairns, as well as crabs and lobsters. The little hamlet even had its own cod-liver oil factory.

Baiting the long lines with mussels and limpets collected from the foreshore was a labour-intensive job, and the whole family was often enrolled to help. Wooden boxes, such as the one in the foreground, were floated just below the surface of the water and used to store live lobsters and crabs. The boat-shaped wicker basket to the right is called a 'scull', and the baited lines were laid on wooden slats inside the basket called 'lintries' (line trays). Grass was put between the lines to prevent the hooks from catching on each other.

Cove fishermen prepare to launch one of their boats, attaching hemp ropes to the hull before hauling it over rough wooden rollers to the water's edge. Cove's original harbour was begun in 1770 and finally completed in 1831. The author of the *New Statistical Account* of *c.*1840 said of the village: 'So perfectly secluded is this little bay and so unexpected is the scene which almost instantaneously opens to the view, that it produces on the mind of the stranger an almost electrical effect of surprise and admiration'.

Cove fishermen tend their nets on the beach, removing seaweed and other debris, and repairing holes in readiness for the next fishing trip. In the background there are open-decked boats and a salmon coble, with nets hung out to dry on posts beyond it. The derelict building is now a private house.

The Victorians were great amateur naturalists, and many combed the coastline of Berwickshire, exploring its rock pools. This rock, called the 'Standalanie', and the surrounding shallow pools, were features of a favourite coastal walk between Cove and Pease Bay, but could only be visited at low tide.

Pease Bridge, above the dene at Pease Glen, was built in 1772. It is one of the highest bridges in Scotland, and traverses a deeply etched valley with a stream at the bottom of it. The Scottish Wildlife Trust now look after part of the ancient forest in this valley, which contains footpaths leading all the way down to Pease Bay, past where the former mill once stood.

Pease Mill, now demolished, was in active use until at least 1943. The mill lade, which supplied water to the wheel, runs along the elevated channel visible at the left hand edge of the mill. A fete is taking place in the background.

Pease Bay before the introduction of the caravan park, with two farmers crossing the burn at a rough ford which cuts across the beach. They would have been collecting washed up seaweed for use as fertiliser.

REMAINS OF FAST CASTLE, COCKBURNSPATH

References to Fast Castle date back to as early as 1333. The castle changed hands many times, and was taken over by Sir Patrick Home, fourth son of the first Lord Home, in 1487. Margaret Tudor stayed there on her way to marry King James IV in 1503. The castle's most infamous owner was Robert John Logan, the seventh and last Baron Restalrig who, along with the Earl of Gowrie, was involved in 'The Gowrie Conspiracy', a plot to assassinate James VI. Logan was described at the time as being 'ane godles drunkin and deboshit man' and had several writs against him for treasonable behaviour. It was not until nine years after his death that his role in the conspiracy was established. His body was exhumed from within the walls of Fast Castle and taken to the High Court in Edinburgh, where his bones were tried for treason and sentenced to death!

PETTICURWICK, St ABBS

South of Fast Castle lies Lumsdaine shore, where legend has it that witches once gathered around the grey stane and danced nine times 'wither-shins' (counter clockwise). The old salmon station at Pettico Wick, beyond Lumsdaine, was once thriving. The wooden storehouse in the centre is part of an old upturned boat. In ancient times, the monks of Coldingham Priory who took much of this catch would never utter the word salmon, referring to it simply as 'that fish'. There were many such ancient superstitions connected with fishing and sailing; for instance, it was considered unlucky for a woman to board a fishing boat.

The slipway at Pettico Wick was constructed by the Northern Lighthouse Board to service the lighthouse at St Abb's Head before the road to St Abbs village was built. This photograph was taken by Robert 'Robbie' Nisbet, who was the postmaster at St Abbs for many years. The lighthouse board's coastal supply ship *Pharos* could only use the slipway to land supplies between half and full tide.

LANDING STORES, ST. ABBS.

Brightly beams our Father's mercy
From his lighthouse evermore;
But to us, he gives the keeping
Of the lights along the shore.

The sight of the SS *Mauretania* undergoing sea trials off St Abb's Head must have been quite breathtaking. The lighthouse, with foghorn, became operational in 1862 and was manned continually until a few years ago. Technology has now overtaken tradition, and the lighthouse is fully automated. The *Statistical Account* of c.1790 states that the local fishermen collected eggs and young seabirds from the cliffs around St Abb's Head. The eggs were good, but the flesh of the seabirds was not, although it helped to sustain poorer families.

St. Abbs from West

At one time most of the village of St Abbs was owned by the Usher family of Usher Vaux Breweries, although there have never been any licensed premises there. The large building in the foreground is Northfield House, once the home of Andrew Usher Esq., Laird of Northfield and St Abbs. A small harbour was built at 'Northfield Shore' in 1833 at a cost of £1,200, when sixteen families lived close by. Records of 1834 tell of fourteen fishing boats using the harbour and their catches being transported in carts to the markets in Edinburgh. The village was known as Coldingham Shore at the time, and connected to Coldingham by an old fisherman's path called the Creel Path.

St. Abbs from Harbour

Another view published by Robbie Nisbet, showing fishing yawls waiting for the tide to turn before leaving for the Hebrides, Orkneys and Shetlands. The floats on board were made from animal bladders. This is a particularly old picture and shows the harbour before the lifeboat slipway was built.

We left our sweethearts and our wives,
A-weeping on the pier;
Cheer up, my dear, we shall soon return,
For it's only half a year.

This postcard was sent to Hobart, Tasmania, in August 1905 and clearly shows snow on the ground – unusual for the Berwickshire Coast. The picture is of Isabelle Cowe wearing the traditional garb of Scottish fish wives. Isabelle and her sisters had the St Abbs Haven Hotel built. The traditional cry of the fish wives was 'Caller Herrin''. Fishing was a dangerous business, and frequently cost the 'lives o' men':

Wha'll buy my herrin'?
They're no' brought here without brave darin'!
Buy my caller herrin'?
Ye little ken their worth.
Wha'll buy my herrin'?
Oh, ye may ca' them vulgar farin',
Wives and mithers maist despairing
Ca' them lives o' men.

" Caller Herrin' "—St. Abbs Fishwife   H.H.H.

This group of 'Shore' fisherwomen, with Isabelle Cowe in the centre of the photograph, are posed in front of the local church. Formerly known as Coldingham Shore, St Abbs is now named after Ebba, the fourth daughter of one of the Kings of Northumberland who established a nunnery on the headland around the year 660.

St. Abbs Lifeboat after the Launch.

A HOLIDAY EXPERIENCE
AT
ST. ABBS.

Have arrived here. Got a splendid place to stay at. Everything O.K. and there is no "Cod" about our Menu.

Herrings kippered, herrings broiled,
Herrings salted, herrings boiled;
Herrings fried, and herrings potted,
Herrings to every meal allotted;
Herrings red and herrings white,
Herrings morning, noon, and night;
Herrings large and herrings small,
So come, dear friend, and taste them all!

Believe me

Your long-lost Kipper,

L v 19 Copyright.

St Abbs' first lifeboat, *Helen Smitten* (No. 603), was launched on 25 April 1911. The legacy of Mr James Hodge of Manchester, she cost £3,563 and was bought as a direct result of the sinking of the *Alfred Earlandsen* on the treacherous Ebb Carrs, near to St Abbs. The lifeboat worked from the harbour for 25 years and saved 37 lives, serving the village and its fishermen until 1936. The modern lifeboat is of the inshore variety, housed in a covered shed directly behind where the lifeboat is situated on the slipway.

Who will man the life-boat? Who the storm will brave?
Many souls are drifting, helpless on the wave . . .

This is typical of the mass produced postcards that were published at the turn of the century for most Scottish coastal villages. The publishers simply changed the photograph and the name of the town. This one, produced in 1911, shows the launching of the lifeboat *Helen Smitten*, yet the rhyme is about herring.

This pre-1890 picture shows St Abbs before the inner harbour walls and pier were built. The fishing yawls and salmon cobles or 'punts' are pulled up onto a shoulder of gravel foreshore which ran up to the first of the houses, once known as Under Row. The horse and cart collected the fish from the boats at low tide.

A later picture showing St Abbs harbour proper. Rock House, right, was built to replace the older building in the upper picture which was destroyed by a storm. The rough stone wall to the left is common to both buildings.

Villagers outside the cottages of Under Row, St Abbs. These were built c.1785, and were subsequently demolished to provide a car park. Before the advent of running water every cottage had a barrel for collecting rain. Hemp ropes, such as those in the right foreground, were used on the fishing boats and got incredibly heavy when wet, requiring constant drying out. When this picture was taken the village was still called Coldingham Shore.

The fishermen's cottages of Upper Row, located on the cliff-top looking over the harbour, were built in 1837 and still stand today. They were built to a traditional Scottish design featuring a wide central chimney and were familiarly known as 'clat and clay' houses. This row now forms part of Seaview Terrace.

After salmon and herring, fishing for lobsters was the other mainstay of St Abbs' economy. These three worthies were photographed next to the huts at Under Row. The gentleman on the left bears a striking resemblance to my good friend and lifeboat coxswain, Alastair Crowe, although unfortunately there is no one alive today to accurately identify the men.

Fishermen, sitting on herring barrels, mend their nets. An old salmon coble or 'punt', cut in half and raised on blocks, serves as a protective shed for their fishing equipment. Some of these upturned boats were even used as houses.

A group of fishermen at the bottom of the brae, St Abbs, photographed in 1892 after a mussel collecting expedition. Mussels were collected in baskets and transferred into a wheelbarrow. The hats are typical of those traditionally worn by fishermen, as is the gentleman on the right's beard, which is only worn under the chin and not on the face.

Once the men had collected them, the womenfolk set to 'sheelin' th' mussels' and baiting the long lines. Each of these had hundreds of hooks, and after being baited they were laid on the 'lintries' of the shallow wicker baskets or 'sculls'. Long lines were used to catch both 'round fish', such as haddock, cod, ling and hake; and flatfish, including flounders, dab, sole, turbot, and the king of the flatfish, the halibut. The baited lines also caught various species of skate and ray. A typical small (inshore waters) line would carry 600 – 1000 hooks attached to the main line or 'back' by 'snuids' spaced three feet apart. The snuid was part line, part plaited horse hair. The 'tippin', to which the hook was attached, was secured by thread. Long lines were used almost exclusively until the introduction of purse seines and trawl nets.

Before we leave St Abbs, I thought it interesting to show another aspect of the village with this picture of the former tennis courts near the church and school. With the influx of tourists into the area from the 1920s onwards, many houses in St Abbs began to offer bed and breakfast. The new leisure seekers are scuba divers, exploring the life underneath the waves.

ST. ABBS FROM THE AIR

A final view of the village with Under Row, next to the harbour, still standing. The lifeboat has a protective shed, but the harbour wall in the foreground has yet to be extended, and the inner slipway has not been built to the low water line.

1st August to 1st October 1917.

St. Abb's Haven.

The St Abbs Haven is the first large building encountered as our route continues southwards towards Coldingham Bay and Sands. Built for Isabelle Cowe and her sisters (page 15), it was a private residence until the sinking of the *Titanic* on 15 April 1912. The sisters were so taken by the plight of the children whose parents had been lost on the liner that they converted the Haven into a home and fostered children there for many years. The Haven also took in paying guests, and was popular with wealthy visitors who came to take the sea air and enjoy the gardens and magnificent view. Over the years it expanded with the addition of a new wing, until it eventually became the St Abbs Haven Hotel. A license to sell alcohol was issued for the first time in the St Abbs Parish, although there are still no licensed premises in St Abbs proper.

THE LOUNGE

The interior of the main lounge of the Haven, illustrating its turn of the century splendour, with wood panelling and an open gallery leading to the bedrooms. With fine palms and rich furniture, the hotel was indeed a haven for its visitors. This painting of St Ebba, the 'White' or 'Grey Lady', was stolen when the hotel stood derelict for a number of years. St Ebba established a nunnery on the headland in the seventh century. It is said that when the nunnery, perched high on St Abb's Head, was about to be overrun by Norse invaders the nuns mutilated themselves to make themselves less attractive, and literally 'cut off their noses to spite their faces'. It is said that the ghost of St Ebba can still be seen moving around on the top landing!

This postcard of Coldingham Sands was published by A.R. Edwards and Son of Selkirk, probably the most prodigious producer of postcards of the Borders at the turn of the century. The postcard was available for many years, and while subsequent versions showed the same scene, alterations were made such as removing the pram and painting in more grass. An earlier version shows a pair of shoes beside the pram – they have been painted out in this card! The Sands are still very popular today; this picture shows them with tents for changing in and a few beach huts. The imposing building at the top of the hill is The Mount.

This building, with splendid views over the Berwickshire coastline, became a convalescent home in the early 1900s. During the First World War the home was called Manderston Hospital. The building and its grounds are now owned by the Youth Hostel Association.

The upper postcard, sent in 1904, shows Coldingham Sands with only one house, Sea Neuk, at the top of the brae. Over the next few years half a dozen more buildings, including the Haven Hotel and Dunlaverock, were built on the brae, which offered superb views. The popularity of Coldingham Sands warranted the two cafés and proliferation of bathing huts. It is said that when St Columba visited Coldingham Priory he bathed at the sands at midnight whilst 'otters and other sea animals played around his feet'. Fortunately otters can still be seen in the area, but they are very rare.

333. BANK TOPS, COLDINGHAM.

These photographs, taken on 28 August 1916, show the wreck of a 'Coastal' class First World War airship, C.16.
Measuring 196 feet in length, with a capacity of 170,000 cubic feet, this monster went into free-balloon descent at the north
end of Coldingham Bay after both her engines failed. The ship was completely destroyed, although no lives were lost.
When fully loaded, airships such as C.16 could carry almost half a ton of bombs, travelling at a maximum speed of about
47 m.p.h. An intriguing feature included an upper gun platform (for protection of the airship), which was accessed by a
30" diameter tube that passed through the centre of the sausage-shaped balloon, and terminated in a wooden trapdoor
near the top. The writing on the Humbie Knowe (the small hill in the background) reads 'Hill 60. Mons, St Eloi, Ypres,
Loos, Somme, Mone.'

Pilgrims on the shore of Coldingham Bay holding the Service of the Sea. This card was sent from Ayton to Reston, only a couple of miles away, on 23 August 1905. At the turn of the century, the majority of postcards were only sent a short distance. Their recipients would be sure to get them the next day, and with few telephones this was an ideal way to communicate.

Fishers Brae in Coldingham has changed little over the years. Prior to the expansion of St Abbs village from 1837 onwards, most local fishermen lived in the brae. They walked the Creel Path from here to the Shore. The John Wood collection of photographs was formerly on display on Fisher's Brae. The collection came to light when it was noticed that old glass photographic plates were being used to repair a local greenhouse! It is regarded as one of the finest collections of late Victorian and Edwardian photographs on the east coast.

The Bogan or Bogangreen is within Coldingham but has always had a quite separate identity. It was originally known as Weavers Row and in 1841 54 handloom weavers lived there. Their speciality was gingham. The houses, which are situated on the other side of the burn, have mostly been bought as holiday homes. Early statistical accounts tell of an increase of poverty in the village 'which may be described to the too common use of tea, and the immoderate use of whiskey'.

Coldingham Market Cross, 1918. The water fountain centre left was one of two in the town. An identical one is still to be found at St Abbs harbour, on the way to the lifeboat station. The Anchor Inn, just out of shot to the right, is still one of the most popular pubs in the town.

THE CROSS, COLDINGHAM.

The gentleman on the bicycle is the local postman, his bag probably filled with postcards such as this one! The anchor sign of the inn of the same name can be seen hanging from the wall to the right.

BRIDGE STREET FROM E., COLDINGHAM.

Looking from Coldingham Market Square towards Bridge Street. The children are dressed in their finery, so the photograph was probably taken on a Sunday. The building to the left is the New Inn. At the junction the road leads south to Eyemouth or west to Reston and Ayton.

The view up Bridge Street towards the Market Square, Coldingham, with the postie once again prominent in the picture.

Farmers from Coldingham Law Farm watering their horses, which they would unharness and ride bareback down to this pond. On the coast farmers used to take their horses down to the sea to cool off. A certain John Neil of Tweedmouth was charged with sorcery and witchcraft after meeting his accomplices to conspire and cast spells against Sir George Home of Manderston on Coldingham Law.

Coldingham appears on Ptolemy's Roman map of Britain, where it is called Colania. An alternative source of the name could come from the Saxon *colaunham*, which translates as 'hamlet situated in the cold vale'. Coldingham Priory still dominates the village, which grew up to serve its needs. Mary Queen of Scots was a regular visitor there when her brother John Stuart was prior. During its history the priory has been Roman Catholic, Episcopalian and Presbyterian. The surviving part of it now serves as the parish church of Coldingham.

As far back as the seventh century there was a monastic settlement on Coldburgh (now St Abb's Head). In 679 Bede stated that it was a 'Monastery of Virgins', but the community was known to include monks too. Originally called the church of St Mary Coldingham, and constituted as a cell of Durham, Coldingham Priory was founded by King Edgar in 1098.

In 1509 the priory was disjoined from Durham and placed under the jurisdiction of Dunfermline by the Pope. The Earl of Hertford burned it to the ground in 1545 and it was further ravaged by Cromwell, who left only the north wall and east gable standing. Coldingham Priory was finally repaired in 1831. The interior of the nave is superb and the acoustics are considered to be among the best on the east coast.

At one time the priory had the right of sanctuary, allowing 37 days grace to persons who sought refuge within the prior's domain. Its perimeter was marked by crosses and many of the local farms still bear the name of the cross (for example Whitecross and Cairncross). Coldingham Priory is well worth a visit, and the old graveyard contains some fascinating graves and carvings. The monks held land at St Abbs and Eyemouth for the landing of their supplies, but were not necessarily the benefactors that we think of monks as being today. They essentially controlled the coastline, charging for fishing and farming rights.

The settlements along the Great North Road and railway, such as Grantshouse (above), all played an important role in the coastal villages' lives. Bypassed by the A1 and now largely forgotten, Grantshouse has changed little over the years.

Post Office, Grantshouse

I don't think you have got this view in your collection I think it is a new one. Hoping all well E.W.L.

A view of the old post office at Grantshouse was obviously considered to be a collector's item. We often think of today's collectors when we see old postcards, but we are only just beginners.

The Greenwood Inn at Houndwood, south of Grantshouse, was a popular stopover for travellers using the Great North Road. These buildings stood near the present day sawmill.

548. THE REST TEA ROOMS. HOUNDLAW

Houndwood before the A1 was diverted around the village. The tea room was very popular for many years.

Smithy and railway were both vital to the Berwickshire fishing industry, as the fishermen had to transport their catch by horse and cart to the railway station, from where it was despatched to market. Heughhead Smithy was considered to be the best in the area, servicing all of the local farmers and 'fish cadgers'. This picture dates from *circa* 1924.

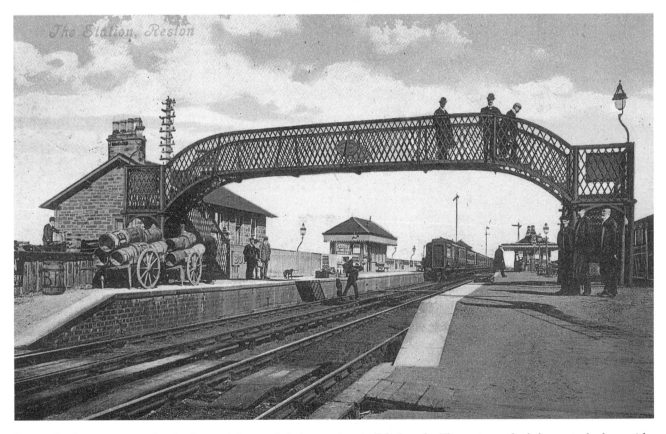

Reston Station was a popular staging post for goods being sent up to Edinburgh. The carts on the left are stacked up with empty fish barrels waiting to be returned to the wholesalers. A train is in the station, but must be at rest as there is someone crossing the line with a load on his back. I guess it was too much effort to take the bridge!

The village of Reston grew up around the needs of the railway. Although the area's cattle market is still centred in the village the train no longer has a scheduled stop, either for goods or passengers.

The next village on the main road south is Ayton, almost two miles due west of Eyemouth. The original name of Eitun is taken from the Saxon words *ei* (water) and *tun* (villa). The village is dominated by Ayton Castle, built in 1851 for William Mitchell-Innes, the former Governor of the Bank of Scotland and the home of the Liddell Graingers since 1885. This picture shows one of the lodge entrances to the castle.

Ayton Station was located to the west of the town where the ground was more suitable for laying track. This picture shows the station-master and porters. Passenger services were withdrawn from Ayton on Monday 5 February 1962, the same day that they ceased at Burnmouth and Eyemouth. It was the end of an era.

Ayton is now largely forgotten, having been bypassed by the A1. This turn of the century picture shows the old town leading towards the police station with its very distinctive clock tower.

Ayton Police Station was built in 1880 and still stands today. The constable (left) is PC Brown, grandfather of Ewan Frater, sign-writer from Ayton and good friend of mine.

Millbank lies along the Eyemouth road, beyond the second entrance to Ayton Castle. At one time there were four flour mills, two paper mills and a brewery in the area. This picture of the old Netherbyres Mill was posted in 1906, although the photograph is much older. Virtually nothing remains of this mill. The old paper mill at Millbank was destroyed by fire in 1869 after being in operation for 61 years. The only paper mill still in existence using the waters of Berwickshire is Dexter's, now situated outside Chirnside.

Netherbyres Mill.

The lodge at the southern entrance to Netherbyres House, on the outskirts of Eyemouth, has been demolished. Netherbyres was the former home of Lt. Colonel Furness, and is now a gardeners' retirement home.

Maggie Murphy's Cottage was situated on a rather tight corner on the Eyemouth side of Millbank, close to Netherbyres Mill. Sadly the building fell into complete disrepair and the roof was finally removed several years ago.

The North British Railway line to Eyemouth travelled downhill all the way from Burnmouth and crossed the River Eye near Millbank. The viaduct was constructed to raise the line 60 feet above the riverbed. There were six 50-foot iron girder spans, supported on brick-faced concrete piers. When the station finally closed, the track was lifted and now only the piers remain. The train in this picture is travelling westwards to the main line terminus at Burnmouth.

The old toll bridge, Eyemouth. Originally the railway terminus was to be located in the field above where Gilsland housing estate now stands. Instead the railway company decided to place the station at the mouth of the river behind the harbour. Their intention was to eventually extend the track onto the quay. The old bridge and toll house have since been demolished to make way for a new bridge and a ring road.

Drooned within sicht o' their hames,
Throttled there doon tae their graves,
Wi' the screams o' their poor wives and weans
Mixed up wi' the crash o' the waves!

Rev. Dr. Walter C. Smith, 1881.

There was weeping on every side, There was na a
hame unbereft;
Fathers, and brothers, and lovers – there was
hardly a man of them left!

The 'Disaster' Memorial Eyemouth.   880

Looking up the Cut towards James Weatherhead's boatyard, with
the station in the background. Beyond is Victoria Road, with only a
few houses built on it. The quayside is stacked with herring barrels;
the wooden structure is a former toilet which offered the bare
necessities for sewage disposal straight into the river. The
significant feature of this photograph, however, is the boat tied up
in the foreground. She is the Berwickshire registered *Ariel Gazelle*,
LH270, the only Eyemouth fishing boat to remain with all her crew
intact after the sudden and devastating storm which struck the east
coast on 14 October 1881. So sudden was the tempest that in all 189
men from the east coast lost their lives. Eyemouth alone lost 20

boats and 129 men, leaving 73 widows and 263 orphans. The *Ariel Gazelle* limped along at sea for 45 hours, her rigging and sails in tatters. She eventually struggled into port on the day her crew's funerals had been scheduled for. Described as a 'funnel of wind', the dreadful 'Euroclydon' was responsible for the destruction of some 30,000 trees at Spottiswood alone. This was a cyclone of truly awesome proportions. As well as the men lost at Eyemouth, 24 were lost at Burnmouth; 15 at Newhaven; 11 at Cove; 7 at Musselburgh and 3 at St Abbs. This event is now known simply as the 'disaster day'.

A disaster memorial was erected by public subscription and was originally placed at the entrance to the graveyard on Coldingham Road. It has now been moved to the old graveyard in the centre of the town. Eyemouth Museum has a superb tapestry depicting the tragedy – now internationally renowned – on permanent display.

A superb book, *An Old-Time Fishing Town – Eyemouth*, by the Rev. Daniel M'Ivor, was published in 1906 and tells the story of the community and those sad days.

Looking east along Victoria Road. The group to the right are sitting on the wall overlooking the railway station and appear to have a laden picnic basket; perhaps they are waiting to catch the train to Burnmouth, or even Berwick. In 1913 25,593 passengers used the line, bringing in a revenue of £2,498; freight charges amounted to £1,628. 34,798 passengers travelled on the line in 1920. A single ticket from Burnmouth to Eyemouth cost thruppence; a return was fivepence. When the line closed in 1962 the fare was 1/6 return.

The view from the old toll bridge. The railway line curves around to the north of the River Eye and terminates just before the harbour. The chimney belonged to the incinerator of the old bone mill, where the carcasses of butchered animals were destroyed. The route of the old railway line is still evident, but is becoming less and less obvious with the passing of time.

A particularly detailed view of the River Eye and Eyemouth Station. Originally the railway company intended to lay track on to the quay, but baulked at the cost of buying the large house which stood in their way. The station remained where it was and local fishermen had to transport their fish up to it by horse and cart. The old wooden footbridge was destroyed during the great flood of August 1948.

The station was officially opened on 13 April 1891. Alterations were made in 1895, and it is believed that the station was destroyed in a fire and rebuilt in 1900. It is unclear whether the station buildings are fire damaged or undergoing demolition in this picture.

Over a twelve year period the Eyemouth Harbour Trust repeatedly tried to gain the land needed to extend the line on to the quay and rebuild the original station. But the expense could not be justified and the station stayed where it was until its closure on 5 February 1962. This fine old photograph is taken from the top of the road leading down into the station, along which all freight was transported.

The station, with a number of goods waggons in the sidings. These were used for transporting fish up to the main line. During winter the line was particularly hazardous as water from the fish boxes used to freeze on the tracks. As the route out of Eyemouth was on a slope this caused a number of accidents.

This picture predates the building of the Eyemouth railway, which was begun in 1885. It shows the banks of the River Eye, photographed from opposite Brown's Bank, a distillery operated by Messrs Calder until 1840. The land beside the river was called the Bane Mill Brae. The smaller 'summer boats', used for shorter journeys, are seen here pulled up on the river bank.

The final bend in the river, before it enters the harbour, is known as the Cut. This old wooden bridge was destroyed in the great flood of 11 August 1948 and was replaced with the 'Silver Bridge'.

THE FLOOD, EYEMOUTH HARBOUR, 12·8·48.   C 6051.

At the height of the storm on the following day the River Eye was in severe spate, overflowing its banks and cascading along the quayside. These fishing boats have been gathered further inside the harbour at half tide to avoid any collision damage by debris. At full tide, you could not tell where the river ended and the harbour began.

AFTER THE FLOOD, EYEMOUTH. 13·8·48.   C 6053.

Another view, this time from the Cut, looking up the river towards the railway station. Trees and other debris have been piled up against the harbour and the bridge has quite clearly been washed away.

Eyemouth Harbour, showing the extended pier in front of Gunsgreen House. At one time there were 27 different smoke houses or smokeries in the town, turning out kippers 'by the mile'. There are now only a couple left, the largest being owned by Ian Waddell. His great grandfather, Robert Waddell, started the business in 1860 after his fishing boat sank because it was so full of herring. His brother was drowned, and vowing never to go to sea again Robert became a very successful fish merchant.

The harbour at the turn of the century, with large stacks of herring barrels and standard fish boxes on the quay. What is probably more interesting to note, however, is the washing hanging out all along the harbour, indicating that this was where people once lived as well as worked, and not just the commercial centre it is today. The large tenement block, known as Glasgow Terrace, was demolished many years ago.

A photograph of Eyemouth's fleet when it was making the transition from yawls to steam drifters. Some of the sailing boats subsequently had paraffin engines fitted. The first one to be converted was the *Maggie James*, BK167, also the first boat to use a seine net rather than long lines. She still holds the record for the largest quantity of herring caught – 230 cran – with one cast or 'shot' of the net. These vessels are waiting for the tide to rise before they negotiate the sand bars and enter the harbour. The tightly packed drifters would return in the order in which they had left: the first into the bay would be the first back into the harbour, and would possibly get the best price for its catch of fish.

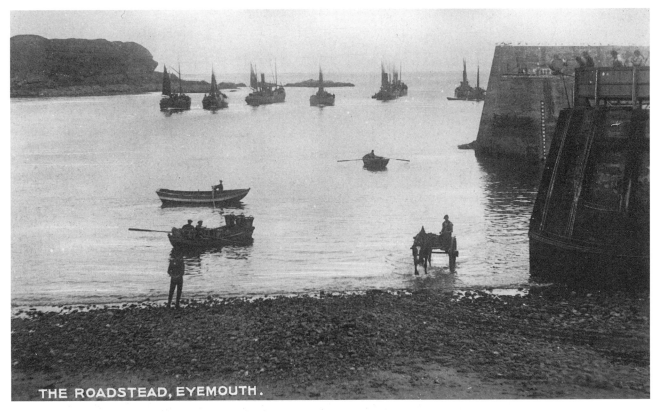

If the tide was low the returning fishing boats and their crews would be marooned in the bay. Rather than wait for the tide to turn, they frequently offloaded some crew – and some of their catch – using small salmon cobles or punts. Here the horse and cart is waiting to off-load the catch ferried in baskets at the stern of the nearest punt. At the time of the disaster in 1881, a fishing boat cost £350 to build.

Yawls in Eyemouth Bay prepare to enter the harbour on an incoming tide. The fishermen often sang religious songs and seafaring shanties as they worked, and *North Sea Shoals* was a popular one:

> *Come all ye jolly fishermen, that plough the rolling sea*
> *The whole year round, and the fishing grounds*
> *On the Northern Minch, on the Norway Deeps,*
> *On the banks and knolls of the North Sea holes,*
> *Where the herring shoals are found.*
> *It's there you'll find the Eyemouth lads.*

Boats crossing the harbour bar, rowing against the flow of the river and furling their heavy cotton sails as they complete the last leg of their journey to the fish market. The original harbour was built in 1746 to accommodate the 150 fishing boats in the port. Following the disaster in 1881 the harbour was widened and deepened, with the work completed in 1885. Improvements included the addition of a new pier at Gunsgreen, designed by the engineer Smeaton. He described Eyemouth as 'lying in the corner of a bay, in which ships can work in and out at all times of the tide, or lie at anchor secure from all winds, except northerly or north-easterly. From this circumstance, its situation is very advantageous'.

Landing herring at Eyemouth. Each basket held approximately 7 stone (98 pounds) of fish, and there were 4 baskets to a cran. From the quayside, the herring were taken by hand cart to the fish gutters and curers further along the harbour at Burgon's Yard. 10,000 barrels of herring were landed each year at Eyemouth from 1809 to 1820, with upwards of 150 boats working from the harbour. The port suffered when the migratory fish moved on down the coast, taking the fleet with them.

Miller Lough, left, and his partner were just two of a huge work-force at the harbour who stacked the fish ready for transportation up to the main line station at Burnmouth. Each box of fish carried the same weight as a traditional wicker basket.

The practice of curing fish with salt was introduced to Scotland by Alexander III in the thirteenth century. The herring were gutted, salted and packed into barrels for shipment, each barrel holding up to 1,000 fish. The work was so hard on the fisher lassies' hands that they had to tie their fingers up in rags due to the cuts and salt ingress into the wounds. Before 1750, there were only six fishing boats registered in the village, but after the first pier was built this immediately increased to sixty and steadily rose as further piers were added.

Once the barrels were filled, the lids were sealed by the 'callants'. They were either despatched to the station or rolled down the dock to await coastal traders, which may have come from as far afield as Russia or Poland. This type of work was akin to slave labour as workers on the quay were not protected by the Factory Act. The fisher lassies worked long hours, often in appalling weather conditions.

These fisher lads and lassies followed the herring fleet as it in turn followed the shoals of herring. The workers travelled from the Shetland Islands to Mallaig, Lowestoft and Great Yarmouth as they serviced the Eyemouth fleet. Although this photograph was not taken in Eyemouth, it shows the crew employed by the fish merchant John Burgon, whose business still exists today. Originally a cooper, John came to Eyemouth from Dunbar in 1911, having married the daughter of the Dunbar fish merchant Tom Craig. His waggons carried the 'kists' of fish workers' clothes as they travelled by train all over the British Isles.

This crew of young fish curers are just about to start their shift. Piece workers were paid a basic wage of 8 shillings a week and between 6d and 8d for each barrel packed. Barrels held approximately 850 – 1000 herring.

Sometimes the fishing boats would be so laden with herring that they filled not only their hold but also the deck. The third verse from the *Net Hauling Song* sums this up:

> It's net after net is pulled
>   from the sea
> With the hauling, the shaking,
>   the one, two and three,
> And the herring that are
>   climbing around your seaboots
> And slithering and sliding down
>   into the shoots.

This is the *Spes Bona*, BK193, with her decks awash with herring. An unlucky vessel, she had to be rescued in a combined effort involving both the St Abbs and Eyemouth Lifeboats on 13 March 1944. Later that year she was lost with all hands off Luff Hard Reef below Fort Point, to the north of Eyemouth Bay.

This amazing scene was played out every weekday in Eyemouth at the turn of the century. Cod caught on the long lines were lain out in rows and fish cadgers or merchants bid for them individually, as opposed to the modern practice of buying boxes of fish or even a whole catch. This photograph was taken outside the Hippodrome, now the Mission to Deep Sea Fishermen. A local rhyme of Eyemouth told by the children of neighbouring villages went thus:

> *Fish-guts and stinkin' herrin'*
> *Are bread and milk for an Eyemouth bairn.*

Eyemouth Harbour, with a coastal freighter loading barrels
of herring for shipment to the south. The sluice gates to
the left of the slipway could be opened when the river was
in flood. Smoked or red herring were sent to Newcastle,
London and Hull; white herring went to Ireland, the Baltic
and the West Indies. Much of the herring curing took place
behind the high wall of Burgon's yard, which has now
been replaced by a car park.

A later picture of the fish sale at Eyemouth quay, produced by R.A. McIvor & Son. Mr McIvor was the chemist in Eyemouth at one time. This display includes some of the oddities of the catch, such as skate, rays and conger eels – which were generally not on housewives' shopping lists. The wooden rectangular boxes in the background replaced the traditional fish baskets.

The auctioneers held the audience in their grasp as they took the bids from the cadgers. Details were noted down in the book as each sale was concluded. The auctioneer in this picture is Davie Cormack (who was known locally as 'Shilling'). The gentleman in the straw hat holding the sale book is John Weatherhead, the owner of the auction business. Once the cadgers had made a purchase, the fish would be gutted and cleaned before being sold to any bystanders.

An early aerial photograph of the entrance to Eyemouth harbour, before either the promenade or the Gunsgreen council houses had been built. The higgledy-piggledy rows of houses with their smoking lums were synonymous with the village. In Chambers' *Picture of Scotland*, it is observed 'that at one time all the people, high and low, young and old, rich and poor, were more or less engaged in smuggling, and no house was built without a view to accommodations for contraband goods. The whole town has still a dark cunning look, is full of curious alleys, blind and otherwise, and there is not a single individual house of any standing but what seems as if it could unfold its tales of wonder.'

The old pierhead next to the slipway onto the beach. This crew have been unable to get their boat on the slipway to remove it for necessary repairs; instead, they have deliberately beached the vessel to carry out the work there and then. The hemp ropes are coiled up ready to be loaded onto the boat. Eyemouth boatbuilder James Weatherhead pioneered the closed deck design that was eventually adopted by Scotland's fishing fleet. He started his business in 1839 and thanks to his pioneering construction methods, Eyemouth's fleet became the first in Scotland to be made up completely of vessels with enclosed decks.

The field in the foreground is now the site of
Eyemouth's swimming pool and leisure centre.
Fishermen once lay their nets out to dry there (some are
visible in the bottom right hand corner of the picture),
while local women washed their clothes at the old well
and bleached their sheets on the grassy banking. At one
time there was a putting green on the field and the local
fair was held there. Beach House still stands, but in this
photograph it has two entrances and was quite clearly
two separate houses at the time. The chimney belongs
to the former gasworks, gas having been introduced into
the town in 1847.

Looking along the harbour towards Gunsgreen House, or the Mansion House as it is often called. The sails on the cart would have been on their way from the sail lofts on the quayside. The top of a set of steps can be seen to the right of the nearest street light. These steps were set into the quay and gave access at low tide to fishing boats moored in the harbour.

This picture shows St Ella's Wynd, which branched off Commerce Street. Swan Court, belonging to the Royal British Legion, now occupies the site. The layout of the houses and streets in Eyemouth was thought to be quite deliberately designed to assist the 'jouking' of local exisemen. At the turn of the century it was said that there was more of Eyemouth underground than there was on the surface. Many of the houses had double walls, interconnecting cellars and steps which lifted out of staircases – in fact every conceivable device for fooling the excisemen or 'gaugers' was to be found in Eyemouth, the smugglers' town. Dealing in contraband goods was called 'coopering', and smuggling or shebeening was a way of life for many.

These fine young men about town were, *back row:* John Luke; Davy Grey (previous owner of my family home, Northburn Farm); Jock Johnston; John Dickson; David Fairbairn. *Front row:* George Robertson; William Patterson; and Archie Fairbairn.

The only exciseman ever to be welcomed into Eyemouth was Rabbie Burns, who had the distinction of being made a Royal Arch Mason there in 1787. The Eyemouth Lodge was founded in 1757. An extract from Burns's diary reads: 'Come up to a bold shore and over a wild country to Eyemouth, sup and sleep at Mr Grieve's. Saturday. Spent the day at Mr Grieve's, made a royal arch mason at St Abbs Lodge. Mr. William Grieve, the oddest fellow – takes a hearty glass and sings a good song. Mr. Robert his brother and partner in trade, a good fellow, but says little. Take a sail after dinner – fishing of all kinds pay tythe at Eyemouth.' (Mr Grieve was a former corn merchant who lived at Beach House). This gentleman is Brother Thomas Patterson, who was made Right Worshipful Master of Masonic Lodge St Ebba No. 70 in 1901, the first fisherman to hold the post.

St Ella's Place, with the masts of the fishing fleet waiting at anchor for the tide to change in the background. The shop in the centre was formerly home to Bob & Meg Black's painting and decorating business.

Gunsgreen House was built by Lord Home, the major landowner in the parish. With its fortified walls and underground cellars, Gunsgreen was reputed to be the centre of Eyemouth's smuggling trade. It was said to have passageways running in all directions beneath it, with secret stairs and interconnecting alleys. Each room had two doors to give the occupant a better chance of escape. Some sources attribute the tower at the top of the hill (visible in the upper picture on page 62) to Oliver Cromwell, although historical evidence has established that this is not the case. For many years the tower was used as a dovecote for the big house.

The watch house in the corner of the old cemetery was built from gravestones, and when Burke and Hare were active in the Eyemouth area a constant vigil was kept at the graveyard against the 'body snatchers'. At one time the graveyard was at the same level as the high street, but when a cholera epidemic devastated the town in 1849, killing 100 locals, the unprecedented decision was taken to raise its level to accommodate the extra bodies. The new cemetery was opened in 1885.

There used to be two annual fairs held in the town's market square, one on the first Thursday in June and one on the last Thursday in October. Sadly the markets eventually ceased, but the tradition of exchanging gifts on the last Thursday of October continued for many years. Here Eyemouth folk walk down to the harbour with sails and kists for the boats.

321. THE SQUARE. EYEMOUTH.

This postcard was sent in 1943, not long before the cobbled streets were paved. The shop to the left was once a butcher's owned by my grandfather, Wullie ('Daddy') Dougal. Cobbles have been reintroduced in the last couple of years.

Market Place, Eyemouth

Dougall's, opposite my grandfather's shop, is still in business, but the shop has undergone many changes. The ladies in the background have traditional fishwives clothes on and the fishermen are carrying sculls, used to hold the lines and hooks for the long line fishing. Armitage's shop, to the right, is now a private house.

Market Place, Eyemouth

This picture was taken a few years after the previous one, and shows an expanded Dougall's with a wider frontage and new doorway. Much of the storage space still used by the shop was originally smugglers' cellars which connected many of the buildings close to Eyemouth Harbour to each other.

Church Street, Eyemouth

Having one's picture taken was once a rare event, and the photographer has drawn a crowd for this shot of Church Street. Although not written until the twenties, the message on this postcard tells of the 1881 disaster. The writer also says that herring cost between 10/- and 15/6 per cran at the time.

Looking down Church Street towards the market place. The gateway on the right led to the old church, now Eyemouth Museum. The large building right of centre is the Masonic Lodge St Ebba No. 70.

The 'prefabs' were built after the war and were occupied for many years. Since this picture was taken the bridge has been replaced, the toll house demolished, and the prefabs upgraded into a modern housing development. The toll for a carriage used to be thruppence. This is now a very busy crossroads, and mothers wouldn't dare to walk down the middle of the road pushing a pram anymore.

This rather sweet photograph was produced as a picture postcard for the mums of these young members of an Eyemouth dancing group around 1925. They are, back row: Nessie Lough; Mary Maltman; my mother, Barbara Dougal; Connie Collin; Margaret Collin. Front row: Mary Cowe; Isa Gillie; Nancy Davenport; Margaret McIntosh; and Jean Collin.

The view beyond Gunsgreen has now been irrevocably altered by yet another harbour extension. The entire flat grassy area has been excavated to make a deep water harbour for some of the larger fishing boats, the existing harbour has been dredged and new breakwaters constructed. A new lifeboat station and permanent docking for the town's lifeboat has been provided at the foot of Gunsgreen House.

The Red Hills, Eyemouth. 12038

The Red Hills from the top of the Killiedraughts. A public footpath popular with the townspeople leads from Eyemouth to Killiedraughts Bay and onwards to Linkim Shore and Coldingham Sands. The field dotted with stooks of corn awaiting the threshing machine is now the site of modern caravan holiday homes and chalets, Eyemouth Holiday Park, owned and operated by the Wood family. The walk 'roond the braes' was described as early as the eighteenth century as 'being a tonic to city people'.

261. EYEMOUTH BAY AND POINT.

There was once a very famous fortress on the promontory overlooking Eyemouth Bay. It was built in 1547 by the Duke of Somerset, but demolished after only three years as a result of the Treaty of Boulogne. The Duke of Northumberland had it rebuilt with the help of the French ambassador D'Oysel, but history intervened again and the fort was demolished as part of the Chateau-Cambresis peace treaty between Scotland and England. A body of 3,000 men dismantled it in 60 days, and much of the facing stone was taken to Berwick and used for the construction of the town's walls. What was left was used by Smeaton when he constructed the old harbour wall.

I stood upon the Eyemouth Fort,
And guess ye what I saw?
Fairnieside and Flemington,
Newhouses and Cocklaw
The fairy folk o' Fosterland,
The witches o' Edincraw
The rye rigs o' Reston,
And Duns dings a'.

By 1949 the old sea wall had fallen into such a state of disrepair that a new wall and promenade had to be built. Up until then holidaymakers had to contend with climbing over the collapsed masonry. This picture was taken before the new harbour entrance was built.

When this picture was taken the sea wall at the end of the beach was in such a poor state that it had to be shored up with wood. The old pierhead and coble house are evident, as are the many masts of the fishing fleet in the background. The beach was, and still is, very popular.

This postcard was sent two weeks after the storm it depicts, and illustrates how severely storms can affect the front of the town. No wonder the sea walls were forever being knocked down. Even though the Hurkur Rocks served as a natural breakwater, the waves still pounded in and the houses along the seafront were regularly inundated with water. Their occupants often had to move their belongings out of the houses as a storm approached.

The *Jacob George*, a Yarmouth registered fishing boat, failed to negotiate the difficult entry into the safe haven of Eyemouth harbour in the early 1940s. Skippered by Andrew Dougal ('Old Youngster'), she was driven on to the rocks and eventually wrecked. The crew were rescued by the local coastguard and lifeboat services with the use of a breeches-buoy. This rescue apparatus is made up of a buoy with canvas breeches for the user's legs. The buoy supports the person being rescued as they are pulled to safety with a rope. The technique is demonstrated in this picture, one of three postcards that were produced showing the shipwreck.

Storm, Eyemouth 12.3.06.

The coastal freighter SS *President* struck Whup Ness to the south of the last hole at Eyemouth Golf course on 29 April 1928. She was completely destroyed, but thankfully with no loss of life. Little remains of her now other than a few broken and rusting plates, festooned with all manner of marine life.

The steam drifter *Mauretana* ran aground on the Hurkur Rocks in the early 1930s. Stuck fast, she broke her back on the next tide and was utterly destroyed. Little remains of her except the boilers, which are resting 12 metres below the merciless waves.

THE LIFEBOAT, EYEMOUTH.

The *James and Rachel Grindley* was the first lifeboat to be stationed at Eyemouth and operated from 1876 to 1888. She was built at a cost of £275 thanks to a legacy from Mr Thomas Grindley of Edinburgh. A second vessel with the same name was in use from 1888 to 1901. The lifeboat station was opened in 1876 at a cost of £500. In 1908 it was rebuilt, and a new slipway constructed at a further cost of £750.

And here's to the lads so courageous, so daring,
Who are living their lives way out on the brine,
Transportin' oil and a fishing the herring,
And here's to the lads of the RNLI.

(Chorus of Fraserburgh Lifeboat).

The *Sarah Pickard* (1901-1909), Eyemouth's third lifeboat, was propelled by rowing and had to be hauled out of the water by hand. Stationed at Eyemouth for eight years, she was launched eight times. She was succeeded by the *Ann Francis* (1909-1937). It was only after the arrival of the *Frank and William Oates* at Eyemouth in 1937 that a caterpillar tractor was used to haul the boat up the ramp and into the lifeboat house. The house was demolished as part of the new harbour development.

With lines attached, the crew of the lifeboat try to secure this drifter. Richard Lewis, secretary of the RNLI in 1850, stated that the essential qualities of lifeboats were 'extra buoyancy; self-baling; ballasting; self-righting, stability; speed; storage room and strength'.

The Burnmouth fishing boat *Nellie Wilson*, BK102, photographed at Great Yarmouth. The herring fleet followed the fish south, and several boats from the same port would usually fish together; the vessel behind the *Nellie Wilson* is probably also Berwick registered. The well dressed gentleman with the watch chains is likely to have been the boat's agent, whose job it was to handle the sale of the catch and organise the crew's supplies.

The Gorge, Burnmouth.

884

The gorge or glen at Burnmouth, more commonly known as 'the brae', formed a natural protective inlet which was augmented by a harbour, completed in 1879. Only a few boats now work out of this very picturesque port, and those mainly at the 'poos' (crabs) and lobsters. The difficulty of the descent is amply compensated for by the view; the village and harbour has the appearance of a Cornish fishing village.

STONEFAULDS BURNMOUTH

The road twists and turns quite sharply as you travel 'doon the brae'. The church and former coastguard houses stand at the last corner before the final descent to the harbour. This postcard was sent in 1912 to the coastguard station at Sutton-on-Sea, south of the Humber near Mablethorpe in Lincolnshire. The row of houses on the right, old fishermen's cottages, have long since been demolished.

Fishing boats at Burnmouth, secured in the inner harbour for additional protection and overlooked by the coastguard station. A few summer boats and salmon cobles have been pulled up on the side of the hill. A building, with what appear to be wooden sheds beside it, is just visible in the background between the leftmost two masts. It has been suggested that this building held a lifeboat, but there is no official record of this.

The wooden sheds next to the old 'lifeboat house' actually turn out to be upturned fishing boats, sawn in half and used as houses.

The old harbour at Burnmouth stacked with herring barrels, perhaps waiting to be collected and taken to Ireland by the *Mary Jane Gregory* from Dublin, a vessel that called at the port. Lower Burnmouth ('Doon the Brae') was made up of three separate hamlets: Partanhall (above, background); Ross, next to the harbour; and Cowdrait, at the southern side of the bay. The village which grew up around the railway station was known as Flemington or Upper Burnmouth.

The Leith registered fishing boat, the *Success*, photographed at Burnmouth. She was one of the fleet which travelled regularly down the coast to Yarmouth, keeping her crew away from home for many months at a time. A fisherman was never fully dressed without a hat, and it was the fashion to wear different ones at different times. Varieties included a silken cap; the 'rakie step', which was worn at an angle; and a blue bonnet which was shaped something like a bulky tam-o'-shanter, but drawn up at the top and with a blue tassle attached. Another alternative was a 'cutter' hat, made of straw with a flat glazed top. Gradually high hats such as the cutter were replaced by sealskin caps, similar to Breton fishermen's caps.

These Burnmouth women are at the washing, agitating clothes in the wooden barrels and boiling up pots of water. Early photographs such as these provide a vignette into a way of life most of us will never have a true appreciation of.

Ross and Cowdrait, to the south of the narrow road which hugs the foot of the cliffs past Burnmouth Harbour, were often isolated by the sea, which cut into the headland causing landslides. The shore line is so rocky on this stretch of coast that fishing boats could only be launched or hauled up at high tide when the sea was flat calm.

There is a peace and tranquillity 'Doon the Brae' which echoes that of many of the Berwickshire villages. The last cottage at Cowdrait is now a net store used by a local fisherman.

Upper Burnmouth is still home to the Flemington, either the last or first pub in Scotland, depending on which direction you approach it from. The Flemington cottages have changed little over the last century. They derive their name from the Flemish settlers (originally from Flanders) who came here after being thrown out of England. They were the first to introduce sheep and weaving into the Scottish Borders.

THE STATION, BURNMOUTH.

873

Burnmouth Station at the turn of the century, with passengers waiting on the northbound train. The photograph is rare because it has two trains in the frame. The line to the left was used by the Eyemouth train.

BURNMOUTH STATION

Burnmouth Station with the Eyemouth branch line to the left. This was known as the 'Eight Minute Link', as it only took eight minutes to travel between the stations. There was, however, a delay at Burnmouth where the waggons of fish were transferred to the major north-south line, operated by the Great Northern Railway.

Greystonlees Farm is on the other side of the A1 from the Flemington, but little is known about the tennis courts which were once in Burnmouth.

These buildings at Lamberton Toll, on the border between Scotland and England, no longer exist. This 1880 picture was sent in 1908.

"GRETNA OF THE EAST."
LAMBERTON TOLL AND OLD MARRIAGE HOUSE.   270

LAMBERTON TOLL IN 1880

A PAGE OF ANDREW LYONS REGISTER. 1880.

TOLL HOUSE
ORIGINAL MARRIAGE
HOUSE FOR EAST OF
SCOTLAND.

AT LAMBERTON, NEAR BERWICK ON TWEED

Hailed as the Gretna Green of the Eastern Marches, Lamberton's fame began with the marriage of Princess Margaret Tudor to James IV in 1503, when the bride was handed over to the Scottish King's Commissioners there 'without any expense to the bridegroom'. Lamberton is thought to have had the first horse-racing course in Scotland, dating from the same period. The pages of this register record the marriages of Robert Cambell to Mary Douglas; Walter McCollock to Mary Anderson; John Stuart to Jane Schofield; David Dodds to Anne Rodgers; John Flanaghan to Susan Anderson and John Allen to Jane Steuart.

Lamberton was once much more popular for runaway marriages than Gretna Green. The Temple of Hymen and the Old Blacksmith's Shop, similar to the ones at Gretna, stood witness to a romantic age, but have sadly gone in favour of a dual carriageway. It is hoped that there will be a new cross border development here in the future – with perhaps another marriage house!

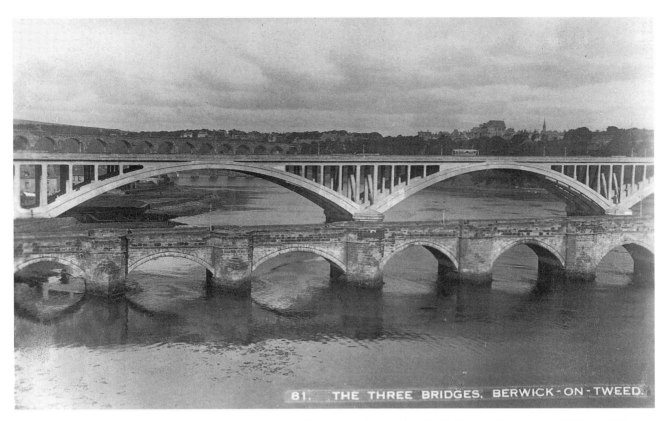

The three bridges over the River Tweed. Uppermost is the 720 yard Royal Border Bridge, built between 1847 and 1850 and designed by Robert Stephenson. In the centre is the Royal Tweed Bridge, opened in 1928. The lower bridge, now known as the 'Old Bridge', was built in 1624.

The Royal Border Bridge was opened on 29 August 1850 by Queen Victoria. 2,000 men were employed in the construction of this twenty-eight arched bridge which stands 138 feet above the river and cost £253,000 to build. The bridge completed the continuous railway link between Edinburgh and London. This picture shows a reunion of people who were present at the bridge's opening. It was perhaps arranged to celebrate the 50th anniversary of this event in 1900.

H.R.H. The Prince of Wales at Berwick.
16th, May 1928. No. 6.

The Royal Tweed Bridge was opened in 1928 by Prince Edward, Prince of Wales, seen here crossing the Old Bridge on 16 May 1928. The new bridge formed part of the A1 trunk road until the town was bypassed in 1983.

ENGLAND. SCOTLAND.

ROYAL TWEED BRIDGE, BERWICK.

This commemorative photograph, taken on the day of the Royal Tweed Bridge's dedication, features the bridge covered in bunting and the bronze coats of arms of Scotland and England. These are situated at their respective ends of the bridge.

Built near the site of a wooden bridge erected in Tudor times but destroyed during the flood of 1607, the Old Bridge was completed in 1634 and cost £15,000. The bridge is 1,164 feet in length and 17 feet wide. Wages at the time of the construction of the bridge were in the region of 6d per tide (work could only be carried out at low tide) for masons, 8d for quarrymen and 4d for labouring women.

This picture of the Royal Border Bridge illustrates what an impressive view passengers would have had as their train crossed the River Tweed. The Flying Scotsman was probably the most famous of the trains which linked Edinburgh with London, and today's Great North Eastern Railway still promotes the line by using its name. The bridge is still in constant use, but its appearance has been altered with the addition of gantries every few yards following the electrification of the line.

An early photograph of the original Berwick Station, built between 1844 and 1846. This was the terminus of the North British Railway Company's Edinburgh to Berwick line.

This photograph is believed to show Berwick Station before it was rebuilt in 1927.

At one time Berwick-upon-Tweed was surrounded by high walls, designed by the Italian engineer Pontinari and built at a cost of £128,000. They were to act as a deterrent against the French Regent, who was in power in Scotland until 1560, and their cost was said to have been more than Queen Elizabeth spent on all her other fortifications put together.

Berwick's ramparts were built for the protection of the town and provided complete control over the mouth of the River Tweed – although in practice the guns were never fired in anger. This was known as Four Gun Battery or Bramham's Battery, and these mighty walls remain as strong today as when they were built.

The Ness or Pier Gate, situated at the end of Ness Street and Kipper Hill, is one of four gates in Berwick's surrounding walls. Constructed in 1816 to provide access to the site of a new pier and lighthouse which were due to be built, it is the most modern of the four gateways. This picture illustrates a common theme among postcard publishers – representing the cross border links between Scotland and England. One of the small boys is dressed in a kilt; the other in traditional trousers.

> *No eager foe assaults the walls, that round old Berwick stand;*
> *But on the ramparts lovers stroll, and gaze o'er sea and land.*

Sallyport lies about three quarters of the way along Bridge Street as you head towards the Old Bridge. This narrow wynd leads down to a gate in Berwick's walls which gives access onto the dockside area, from where fish was transported up to the local shops and market place. The small shop you can see on Bridge street is now an art gallery.

This World War One tank was photographed in front of the statue of James Stuart, outside the guard house at Palace Green. The building in the background was formerly a convent and is now owned by Northumberland County Council. It is used to provide extra classrooms for the older children from Holy Island who have to board when the tides are against their favour.

This row of houses once backed on to the Wallace Green Church. With their sagging pantiled roofs and crumbling walls, it is hardly surprising that they were demolished in the 1920s. A new manse now stands on the site, although the archway to the left is still one of the entrances to the Wallace Green Church.

Postcards of Marygate crop up time and again, and illustrate the historical and social development of the town's main street during the decades following the invention of the camera. This is probably one of the oldest photographs depicting everyday life in Marygate. Hand carts laden with goods are situated where the current market is held. The archway in the background is Scots Gate.

The Town Hall was built between 1750 and 1754 and stands 150 feet high. Its steeple contains eight bells, one of which is an old curfew bell which was formerly rung at eight o'clock every night except Sunday. The statue, depicting the Greek goddess Hygeia, was erected in memory of Dr Philip W. Maclagan. It has since been resited opposite the entrance to the railway station at the top of Castlegate. The Red Lion Hotel is now Boot's the Chemist.

Herring gutting, Berwick-upon-Tweed. Herring gutters such as these worked at every port along the coast. They were mainly itinerant, and travelled with the herring fleet as it followed the shoals of herring. This area of the quayside is now a car park.

Fishing yawls or 'Fifies' moored alongside the Tweed Dock in front of the Old Bridge.

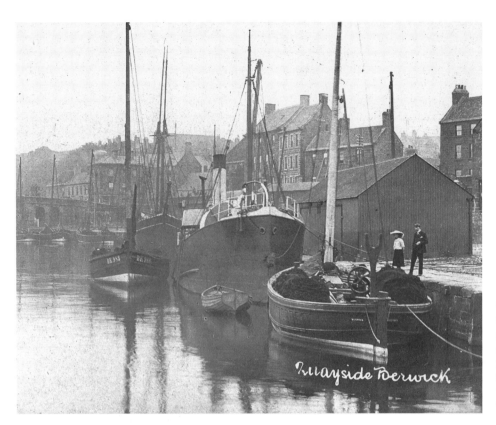

This picture illustrates the transition between old style single-masted wooden boats, driven by wind, and newer motorised steel vessels. Much more efficient, these bigger vessels led to the demise of the wonderful old wooden boats.

These Berwick-registered boats are the *Boy Jacob* and *Emily Read* from Eyemouth. The buildings below the walls have all been demolished and those to the rear and right of the photograph redeveloped as offices and shops. The entrance through the walls to Sallyport lies between the two terraces of buildings on the quay.

The *Border Chief* was one of a number of ferries that operated between Berwick-upon-Tweed and Tweedmouth and Spittal. Another was the *Duke of Windsor*. When the tide was right, small row boats – basically salmon cobles fitted with seats – also acted as ferries. The message on this card, postmarked 11 October 1907, stated that the sender was 'getting on all right. We took over £200 yesterday'. I wonder what the line of work was!

Salmon Fishers, Spittal

*It's busky me lads, get you up on the deck,
And take your stations for hauling the net;
And mind you pull together boys, all through the night,
And sweat in your oilskins until it's daylight.*

Valentine's Series

It seems only fitting to end this journey with a picture of the sea; this one was taken on Spittal foreshore, with the pierhead and lighthouse of Berwick in the background. Salmon are still fished in the same way today, using nets such as these and traditional cobles. The nets are loaded onto the aft of the coble, which is rowed out in a semi-circle allowing the net to run out into the water by itself. On reaching the shore, the net is pulled in and any trapped salmon secured. Until 1788, when it was discovered that ice could be used to store raw fish, the catch was boiled and salted for shipment. Salmon season is from 14 February to 14 September. A popular old rhyme went:

Gae east, gae west, gae north, gae south, there's nocht like Berwick saumon.

ACKNOWLEDGEMENTS

Maj. Gen. Sir John Swinton; Alastair Crowe; Alastair Scott; John Waddell; John Burgon; George Walker; Ewan Frater; Barbara Wood; Lesley Orson; Eyemouth Museum; David Smith, Photographers; St Abbs & Eyemouth Lifeboat Services.

FURTHER READING

Eyemouth in Old Picture Postcards Volume 1, Lawsoon Wood
The Eight Minute Link, A History of the Eyemouth Railway, Lawson Wood
Berwick-Upon-Tweed in Old Picture Postcards, Lawson Wood
An Old-time Fishing Town: Eyemouth - Its History, Romance and Tragedy, Daniel M'Ivor
Berwick, A Short History and Guide, Frank Graham
The History of Berwickshire's Towns & Villages, Elizabeth Layhe

A Farewell at the Borders.